HASHIMOTOS

DIET

COOKBOOK FOR

VEGANS

Discover Delicious Vegan Recipes To Improve Your Thyroid Health And Support Healing!

Laura Osmond

Laura Osmond

Table Of Contents

INTRODUCTION

Mary was disappointed. She had visited the doctor to find out what was wrong after feeling exhausted and rundown for several weeks. It was discovered that her thyroid had been severely damaged by Hashimoto's Disease, an autoimmune condition.

Mary was concerned about how she would treat her ailment despite already following a vegan diet. She had heard harrowing tales of people with Hashimoto's having to give up their favorite meals and adhere to rigid diets.

Mary eventually came across a link to buy this cookbook one day. She was initially skeptical, but the suggestions and recipes seemed good.

Mary took a leap of faith and did what she was told in this cookbook. She started eating a diet higher in fruits and vegetables and lower in processed foods and sugars. She also started practicing yoga and meditation as ways to decompress.

Mary saw the difference within a few weeks. She had more energy, was sleeping better, and felt better all over. Her symptoms had improved tremendously! Because of the delectable recipes in this cookbook, she was able to indulge in her favorite foods without endangering her wellbeing.

Mary can now control her disease and lead a healthy, contented life. She is incredibly thankful to have discovered a cookbook that could guide her in making the lifestyle adjustments she need to regain her best health.

What's Hashimoto's Disease?

An autoimmune condition called Hashimoto's disease, also known as chronic lymphocytic thyroiditis, is brought on by the body's immune system attacking the thyroid gland. The thyroid, an endocrine gland in the neck, creates hormones that control the body's growth, development, and metabolism. The thyroid cells are incorrectly viewed by the immune system as foreign invaders, and antibodies are then produced to combat this perception. Hypothyroidism, a disorder where the thyroid cells are damaged and unable to produce enough hormones, can result from this. In the US, hashimoto's disease is the most frequent cause of hypothyroidism.

Causes Of Hashimoto's Disease

Hashimoto's disease is thought to be caused by a confluence of hereditary, environmental, and lifestyle factors, although the specific etiology is unknown. Research suggests that exposure to specific environmental triggers like viruses and bacteria, as well as a family history of autoimmune diseases, may raise the likelihood of developing Hashimoto's. Hashimoto's disease is also more prone to occur in those with specific genetic alterations, such as the HLA-DR3 gene. In addition, lifestyle factors including stress, a diet high in processed foods, and a lack of exercise can raise the risk of developing the illness.

Symptoms

Symptoms of Hashimoto's Disease can vary from person to person and may include the following:

• **Tiredness:** Feeling tired and weak, even after adequate amounts of sleep.

• Weight gain or difficulty losing weight, even with diet and exercise.

• Dry skin or hair.

• Constipation or digestive issues.

• Joint pain and stiffness.

• Mood changes including depression and irritability.

• Low libido.

• Poor memory and concentration.

• Cold intolerance.

• Muscle aches and weakness.

• Heavy menstrual periods or irregular menstrual periods.

• An enlarged thyroid gland (goiter).

• Elevated cholesterol levels.

• Enlarged lymph nodes in the neck.

• Swelling in the legs and feet.

Diagnosis Of Hashimoto's Disease

A combination of laboratory test and physical examinations are used to make the diagnosis of Hashimoto's Disease. A thyroid-stimulating hormone (TSH) test is the most typical laboratory procedure performed to identify Hashimoto's Disease. The blood thyroid hormone levels are determined by this test. Further tests may be performed to confirm the diagnosis if the TSH level is higher than normal, which may be a sign of an underactive thyroid.

Thyroid antibody tests (looking for antibodies that attack the thyroid using thyroid peroxidase and thyroglobulin antibodies, respectively) and a radioactive iodine uptake test (measuring how much iodine is taken up by the thyroid) may also be used to identify Hashimoto's disease.

To confirm the diagnosis, a thyroid biopsy may occasionally be carried out. A small piece of thyroid tissue is taken during a thyroid biopsy and inspected under a microscope for indications of injury or inflammation.

The most effective course of treatment can be chosen with the aid of the Hashimoto's Disease diagnosis. In addition to lifestyle changes to control symptoms, treatment options may include thyroid hormone replacement medications.

Treatment Options

Treatment for Hashimoto's Disease focuses on controlling the condition's symptoms and getting the thyroid back to normal operation.

Hormone therapy, which involves substituting the hormones the thyroid no longer produces, is the main treatment for Hashimoto's disease. Levothyroxine and other synthetic thyroid hormones are frequently used for this. These hormones assist in reestablishing the body's hormonal equilibrium and aid in easing the illness' symptoms.

To assist in reducing the synthesis of thyroid hormones, doctors may recommend anti-thyroid medications like methimazole. These medications can help to lessen symptoms, but they can also have negative side effects, thus hormone treatment is typically used in conjunction with them.

Rarely, if the thyroid gland is severely damaged, doctors may advise surgery to remove it. This procedure, known as a thyroidectomy, helps lessen the disease's symptoms.

It is significant to remember that treating Hashimoto's Disease involves a long-term process and continual observation. It's critical to visit the doctor frequently to evaluate the disease's development and ensure that the treatment is functioning.

CHAPTER 1

VEGAN DIET GUIDE FOR HASHIMOTO'S DISEASE

The vegan diet for hashimoto's is similar to a regular vegan diet, but with a few adjustments. In this chapter, we are going to take an in-depth analysis of the hashimoto's vegan diet.

Foods To Eat

The ideal strategy for a vegan with Hashimoto's Disease is to concentrate on nutrient-dense, anti-inflammatory meals. Given that Hashimoto's is an autoimmune disease, it's crucial to concentrate on foods that can help the body experience less inflammation.

Concentrate on consuming a lot of fresh produce, especially fruits and vegetables that are strong in antioxidants, such as berries, leafy greens, and cruciferous vegetables (broccoli, cauliflower, Brussels sprouts, etc.). Consuming these foods can improve general health by reducing inflammation in the body.

Include wholesome plant protein sources like nuts, seeds, and legumes. These support a healthy hormone balance and are stocked with vital vitamins and minerals.

Eat avocados, olive oil, and coconut oil to increase the amount of healthful fats in your diet. These can provide your body with essential fatty acids and reduce inflammation.

Eat whole grains like quinoa and buckwheat as part of your diet. These are excellent sources of fiber and complex carbohydrates for long-lasting energy.

As much as you can, try to concentrate on eating organic, unprocessed foods. This can lessen exposure to toxins and other compounds that might otherwise cause the body to become inflamed.

Additionally, be sure to drink plenty of water, which will aid in the removal of toxins from your body and maintain the health of your organs.

In order to alleviate stress and enhance general health, make sure you obtain enough sleep and exercise.

Foods To Avoid

Both foods that can cause an autoimmune reaction and those that can be difficult to digest should be avoided. Processed foods, dairy products, eggs, gluten, sweets, and refined carbs are some of them. Tofu, tempeh, and edamame should also be avoided since they can interfere with the production of thyroid hormones. Last but not least, certain nuts like cashews and peanuts should be avoided because they contain high amounts of lectins that can cause inflammation.

Vegan Nutritional Supplements For Hashimoto's Disease

For a number of reasons, nutritional supplements are crucial for vegans with Hashimoto's disease. In addition to other symptoms, Hashimoto's disease can also induce fatigue, mood fluctuations, and digestive issues. Without the right nourishment, it will be definitely challenging for the body to effectively control the disease's symptoms.

You may not be getting all the vitamins and minerals you need from your diet, but nutritional supplements can help. For instance, you could not be getting enough of the nutrients necessary for optimal thyroid function, such as iron, zinc, selenium, iodine, and vitamin B12. Fatty acids, particularly omega-3 fatty acids, can also support a healthy metabolism and prevent inflammation.

The ideal kind of dietary supplement for you will depend on your specific demands. For instance, a B-complex supplement that includes all the B vitamins as well as iron and zinc can be beneficial for you. A vitamin D supplement may also be something you want to think about since it is crucial for immune system, mood, and bone health. Additionally, you must ensure that you consume enough omega-3 fatty acids, either naturally or through supplements or foods like flaxseed and walnuts. Lastly, be sure to consume enough foods high in fortified plant-based milks, Brazil nuts, iodine, and vitamin B12 to ensure you have enough of these nutrients.

Exercise Techniques To Enhance Your Health

A crucial component of treating Hashimoto's disease is exercise. Exercise can aid in lowering stress and inflammation, both of which can contribute to an escalation of Hashimoto's symptoms. Exercise increases endorphins, which can enhance mood and lessen fatigue.

Low-impact aerobic exercise, such as walking, jogging, swimming, or biking, is the best sort of exercise for someone with Hashimoto's Disease. By engaging in these activities, you can maintain your level of activeness without overworking your body or exacerbating your symptoms. However, you should start out slowly and use light weights when doing strength training. Stop right away and see your doctor if you feel any pain or discomfort. Lastly, stretching exercises like yoga can ease stress and increase flexibility.

Laura Osmond

CHAPTER 2

VEGAN RECIPES FOR HASHIMOTO'S

Recipes For Breakfast

Oats and Almond Butter Porridge

Ingredients:

•half cup of gluten-free oats

•one cup of almond milk

•one tbsp of almond butter

•one tsp of ground cinnamon

•a quarter tsp of sea salt

•a quarter cup of fresh blueberries

Instructions:

•In an average saucepan over medium temperature, put together the oats, almond milk, almond butter, cinnamon and sea salt.

•Stir until the mixture comes to a boil and bring down the heat to low and simmer for five minutes, stirring frequently.

•Take it off the heat and top with fresh blueberries.

•Serve and enjoy!

Prep Time: 5 minutes

Portion Size: 1 bowl

Calorie Count: 385

Quinoa and Apple Breakfast Bowl

Ingredients:

•half cup of cooked quinoa

•half cup of unsweetened applesauce

•a quarter tsp of ground cinnamon

•half cup of unsweetened almond milk

•a quarter cup of chopped walnuts

•a quarter cup of raisins

Instructions:

•In an average bowl, combine the cooked quinoa, applesauce and cinnamon.

•Stir until well combined.

•Add the almond milk and mix thoroughly until everything is evenly distributed.

•Top with chopped walnuts and raisins.

•Serve and enjoy your breakfast!

Prep Time: 5 minutes

Portion Size: 1 bowl

Calorie Count: 395

Coconut Chia Pudding

Ingredients:

•half cup of chia seeds

•one cup of unsweetened coconut milk

•a quarter tsp of ground cinnamon

•one tsp of pure vanilla extract

•a quarter cup of unsweetened shredded coconut

Instructions:

•In a medium bowl, put together the chia seeds, coconut milk, cinnamon and vanilla extract.

•Stir until everything is properly combined.

•Cover and put in the refrigerator for a minimum of one hour.

•Top with shredded coconut and serve.

Prep Time: 5 minutes

Portion Size: 1 bowl

Calorie Count: 488

Baked Sweet Potato Toast

Ingredients:

•one medium sweet potato

•one tsp of ground cinnamon

•one tbsp of almond butter

•a quarter cup of sliced almonds

Instructions:

•Preheat the oven to a temperature of about 400°F.

•Cut sweet potato into 1/2-inch thick slices.

•Place the sweet potato slices on a baking sheet and sprinkle with cinnamon.

•Give it 20 minutes of baking, flipping halfway through.

•Spread almond butter on top of each slice and top with sliced almonds.

•Serve!

Prep Time: 10 minutes

Portion Size: 2 slices

Calorie Count: 195

Avocado Toast with Hemp Seeds

Ingredients:

•two slices of gluten-free bread

•half avocado that's been mashed

•one tsp of ground flaxseed

•one tbsp of hemp seeds

•a quarter tsp of sea salt

Instructions:

•Toast the bread using a toaster or under the broiler.

•Spread mashed avocado on top of each piece of the toast.

•Sprinkle with flaxseed, hemp seeds and sea salt.

•Enjoy!

Prep Time: 5 minutes

Portion Size: 2 slices

Calorie Count: 257

Coconut and Banana Pancakes

Ingredients:

•one cup of gluten-free flour

•one tsp of baking powder

•half cup of unsweetened coconut milk

•half mashed banana

•one tbsp of coconut oil

•one tbsp of maple syrup

Instructions:

•In an average bowl, whisk together the flour and baking powder.

•In another bowl, combine the coconut milk, mashed banana, coconut oil and maple syrup.

•Stir wet ingredients into the dry ones and mix thoroughly until well combined.

•Heat a non-stick skillet over average temperature.

•Scoop a quarter cup of batter onto the skillet and allow for 2-3 minutes of cooking per side.

•Serve and enjoy!

Prep Time: 10 minutes

Portion Size: 4 pancakes

Calorie Count: 280

Green Smoothie Bowl

Ingredients:

• one ripe banana

• half cup of spinach

• half cup of unsweetened almond milk

• a quarter cup of unsweetened shredded coconut

• a quarter cup of chopped walnuts

Instructions:

• In a blender, put together the banana, spinach and almond milk.

• Blend thoroughly until well smooth.

• Pour into a bowl and top with shredded coconut and walnuts.

• Enjoy your smoothie!

Prep Time: 5 minutes

Portion Size: 1 bowl

Calorie Count: 308

Banana Oat Muffins

Ingredients:

•one cup of gluten-free oats

•half cup of almond flour

•one tsp of baking powder

•half tsp of ground cinnamon

•a quarter tsp of sea salt

•a quarter cup of maple syrup

•two mashed bananas

•a quarter cup of unsweetened almond milk

Instructions:

•Get the oven to a preheated temperature of 350°F.

•In an average bowl, you should whisk together the oats, almond flour, baking powder, cinnamon and sea salt.

•In a distinct bowl, combine the maple syrup, mashed bananas and almond milk.

•Pour wet ingredients into the dry ones and mix until everything becomes well combined.

•Use paper liners to line a muffin tin and scoop batter into each cup.

•Give it 20 minutes of baking, or bake until a toothpick inserted into the center comes out clean.

•Serve!

Prep Time: 10 minutes

Portion Size: 12 muffins

Calorie Count: 91

Apple Cinnamon Overnight Oats

Ingredients:

•half cup of gluten-free oats

•half cup of unsweetened almond milk

•a quarter tsp of ground cinnamon

•a quarter cup of unsweetened applesauce

•one tbsp of chia seeds

•a quarter cup of chopped walnuts

Instructions:

•In a medium bowl, put together the oats, almond milk and cinnamon.

•Stir thoroughly until everything is wholly distributed.

•Stir in the applesauce, chia seeds and walnuts.

•Again, stir until everything is properly combined.

•Cover and put in the refrigerator overnight.

•Enjoy!

Prep Time: 5 minutes

Portion Size: 1 bowl

Calorie Count: 315

Tofu Scramble

Ingredients:

•one tsp of coconut oil

•half diced onion

•half diced bell pepper

•half cup of diced mushrooms

•half block of crumbled extra-firm tofu

•one tbsp of nutritional yeast

•a quarter tsp of ground turmeric

•a quarter tsp of sea salt

Instructions:

•Heat coconut oil in a big skillet over average temperature.

•Stir in the onion and bell pepper and cook for five minutes, stirring frequently.

•Include the mushrooms and allow another five minutes of cooking, stirring frequently.

•Add crumbled tofu, nutritional yeast, turmeric and sea salt.

•Cook for five minutes, stirring frequently.

•Serve and enjoy!

Prep Time: 10 minutes

Laura Osmond

Portion Size: 2 servings

Calorie Count: 145

Recipes For Lunch

Roasted Vegetable Quinoa Bowl

Ingredients:

Two cups of cooked quinoa

One chopped red bell pepper

One chopped yellow bell pepper

One chopped zucchini

One chopped yellow squash

One chopped red onion

Two tbsp of extra-virgin olive oil

Two cloves garlic, minced

One tsp of ground cumin

Half tsp of sea salt

A quarter tsp of freshly ground pepper

A quarter cup of chopped fresh parsley

Instructions:

Before you begin, get the oven to a temperature of about 375F.

Place bell peppers, zucchini, squash and onion on a big baking sheet.

Toss with olive oil, garlic, cumin, salt and pepper.

Give 15 minutes of roasting or roast until vegetables are softened and lightly browned.

Serve over quinoa and top with parsley.

Prep Time: 15 minutes, Servings: 4 (242 calories per serving)

Mediterranean Chickpea Salad

Ingredients:

Two cans of drained and rinsed chickpeas

One diced red bell pepper

One-quarter cup of diced red onion

Half cup of diced cucumber

Half cup of halved cherry tomatoes

Two tbsp of extra-virgin olive oil

Two tbsp of freshly squeezed lemon juice

Two tbsp of chopped fresh parsley

One tsp of dried oregano

Half tsp of sea salt

A quarter tsp of freshly ground pepper

Instructions:

In a big bowl, combine the chickpeas, bell pepper, onion, cucumber and tomatoes.

In a little bowl, whisk together the olive oil, lemon juice, parsley, oregano, salt and pepper.

Pour dressing over the mixture of chickpea and toss thoroughly to combine.

Serve instantly or chilled.

Prep Time: 10 minutes, Servings: 4 (190 calories per serving)

Avocado and Bean Wrap

Ingredients:

One whole wheat tortilla

A quarter cup of cooked black beans

A quarter cup of cooked corn kernels

A quarter of mashed ripe avocado

Two tbsp of diced red onion

One tbsp of diced red bell pepper

One tbsp of chopped fresh cilantro

One tsp of extra-virgin olive oil

One tsp of freshly squeezed lime juice

Pinch of sea salt

Instructions:

Spread the mashed avocado onto the tortilla.

Top with beans, corn, onion, bell pepper and cilantro.

Drizzle with olive oil and lime juice and sprinkle with salt.

Roll up the tortilla before cutting in half.

Prep Time: 10 minutes, Servings: 1 (360 calories)

Baked Sweet Potato Fries

Ingredients:

Four big sweet potatoes (peeled and cut into wedges)

Two tbsp of extra-virgin olive oil

One tsp of sea salt

Half tsp of freshly ground pepper

Instructions:

Set the oven to a temperature of about 425F.

Get sweet potato wedges onto a big baking sheet.

Drizzle with olive oil. Then, you can sprinkle with salt and pepper.

Allow 20 minutes of baking or bake until golden brown and crispy.

Prep Time: 10 minutes, Servings: 4 (130 calories per serving)

Roasted Kale and Brussels Sprouts

Ingredients:

One bunch of kale (stems removed and chopped)

One pound of halved Brussels sprouts

Two tbsp of extra-virgin olive oil

Half tsp of sea salt

A quarter tsp of freshly ground pepper

Instructions:

To begin, get the oven to a temperature of 400 degrees Fahrenheit.

Place kale and Brussels sprouts on a big baking sheet.

Toss thoroughly with olive oil, salt and pepper as you wish.

Give it 20 minutes of roasting time or roast until vegetables are lightly browned and softened.

Prep Time: 10 minutes, Servings: 4 (145 calories per serving)

Soybean and Vegetable Stir-Fry

Ingredients:

One tbsp of extra-virgin olive oil

One small onion (chopped)

Two cloves garlic, minced

One chopped red bell pepper

One chopped carrot

One cup of edamame

Two cups of cooked brown rice

Two tbsp of reduced-sodium soy sauce

One tsp of freshly grated ginger

Instructions:

Heat olive oil in a big skillet over average temperature.

Stir in the onion and garlic and cook until tender, about three minutes.

Add bell pepper, carrot and edamame and allow a cooking time of five minutes.

Stir in cooked rice, soy sauce and ginger.

Cook until heated through. This should take about three minutes.

Prep Time: 15 minutes, Servings: 4 (286 calories per serving)

Grilled Portobello Mushrooms

Ingredients:

Four big portobello mushrooms (stems removed)

Two tbsp of extra-virgin olive oil

Two tbsp of balsamic vinegar

One tsp of dried oregano

Half tsp of sea salt

A quarter tsp of freshly ground pepper

Instructions:

Preheat grill to average-high temperature.

Brush mushrooms with olive oil and balsamic vinegar.

Sprinkle with oregano, salt and pepper.

Grill for eight minutes or until softened, turning once.

Prep Time: 10 minutes, Servings: 4 (90 calories per serving)

Lemon and Herb Quinoa

Ingredients:

Two cups of cooked quinoa

Two tbsp of freshly squeezed lemon juice

Two tbsp of chopped fresh parsley

One tsp of chopped fresh oregano

One tsp of chopped fresh thyme

Half tsp of sea salt

A quarter tsp of freshly ground pepper

Instructions:

In a big bowl, combine the quinoa, lemon juice, parsley, oregano, thyme, salt and pepper.

Toss to combine.

Serve and enjoy immediately or chilled.

Prep Time: 10 minutes, Servings: 4 (190 calories per serving)

Beet and Arugula Salad

Ingredients:

Four cups of arugula

One big cooked and diced beet

Two tbsp of extra-virgin olive oil

Two tbsp of freshly squeezed lemon juice

One tsp of maple syrup

Half tsp of sea salt

A quarter tsp of freshly ground pepper

Instructions:

In a big bowl, put together the arugula, beet, olive oil, lemon juice, maple syrup, salt and pepper.

Toss thoroughly to combine, serve and enjoy.

Prep Time: 10 minutes, Servings: 4 (106 calories per serving)

Cauliflower Rice Buddha Bowl

Ingredients:

One head of grated cauliflower

Two tbsp of extra-virgin olive oil

One diced red bell pepper

Half cup of cooked edamame

Half cup of cooked black beans

Two tbsp of chopped fresh parsley

Two tbsp of freshly squeezed lime juice

One tsp of ground cumin

Half tsp of sea salt

A quarter tsp of freshly ground pepper

Instructions:

Get a big skillet over average temperature and heat olive oil in it.

Stir in the cauliflower, bell pepper, edamame, black beans, parsley, lime juice, cumin, salt and pepper.

For about eight minutes, cook, stirring often, until cauliflower is softened and lightly browned.

Serve and enjoy immediately.

Prep Time: 10 minutes, Servings: 4 (320 calories per serving)

Recipes For Dinner

Mediterranean Grilled Eggplant & Zucchini Salad

Ingredients:

- one big eggplant that's been sliced into thin rounds

- one big zucchini (sliced into thin rounds)

- a quarter cup of olive oil

- two tbsp of lemon juice (freshly squeezed)

- two cloves garlic, minced

- half tsp of dried oregano

- half tsp of sea salt

- a quarter tsp of black pepper (freshly grounded)

- a quarter cup of fresh parsley that's been chopped

- two tbsp of chopped fresh mint

- a quarter cup of crumbled feta cheese

Instructions:

1. Preheat the grill to medium-high temperature.

2. Put the eggplant and zucchini slices in a big baking sheet. Drizzle with the olive oil, lemon juice, garlic, oregano, salt, and pepper. Toss thoroughly to coat.

3. Give the vegetables 5-7 minutes of grilling, flipping once, until softened and lightly charred.

4. Move the grilled vegetables to a big bowl. Stir in the parsley, mint, and feta cheese. Toss to combine.

5. Serve and enjoy warm or at room temperature.

Prep time: 10 minutes | Serves: 4 | Calories: 152

Curried Lentil Soup

Ingredients:

- one tbsp of olive oil

Laura Osmond

- one diced onion

- two cloves garlic, minced

- one tsp of ground cumin

- one tsp of curry powder

- one tsp of ground turmeric

- half tsp of ground coriander

- a quarter tsp of ground ginger

- a quarter tsp of ground cinnamon

- 1/8 tsp of ground nutmeg

- two cups of vegetable broth

- one cup of rinsed dried lentils

- two diced carrots

- one diced red bell pepper

- a quarter cup of coconut milk

- two tbsp of chopped fresh cilantro

- Sea salt and black pepper that's been freshly grounded

Instructions:

1. Heat the olive oil in a big pot over average temperature. Add the onion and garlic and cook for five minutes, or cook until tender.

2. Include the cumin, curry powder, turmeric, coriander, ginger, cinnamon, and nutmeg. Cook for just a minute, stirring frequently.

3. Add the vegetable broth, lentils, carrots, and bell pepper. Bring to a boil, then bring down the heat to low and give it 20-30 minutes of simmering, or simmer until the lentils are softened.

4. Stir in the coconut milk and cilantro. Season with salt and pepper to get the desired taste.

5. Serve and enjoy warm.

Prep time: 25 minutes | Serves: 4 | Calories: 294

Roasted Butternut Squash & Kale Salad

Ingredients:

- one little butternut squash (peeled, seeded, and cut into cubes)

- two tbsp of olive oil

- Sea salt and black pepper (freshly grounded)

- four cups of kale (stems removed and chopped)

- two tbsp of lemon juice (freshly squeezed)

- two tbsp of tahini

- two cloves garlic, minced

- a quarter cup of toasted pepitas

Instructions:

1. Set the oven to a preheated temperature of 400° Fahrenheit.

2. Place the butternut squash cubes on a big baking sheet. Drizzle with the olive oil before seasoning with salt and pepper. Toss thoroughly to coat.

3. Roast for fifteen to twenty minutes, or roast until softened.

4. Place the kale in a big bowl before adding the roasted butternut squash.

5. In a little bowl, whisk together the lemon juice, tahini, and garlic. Drizzle over the salad and toss thoroughly to get it combined.

6. Top with the toasted pepitas and serve.

Prep time: 30 minutes | Serves: 4 | Calories: 185

Quinoa Stuffed Peppers

Ingredients:

- four halved and seeded bell peppers

- one tbsp of olive oil

- one diced onion

- two cloves garlic, minced

- one cup of cooked quinoa

- one can of drained diced tomatoes

- half tsp of Italian seasoning

- one-quarter tsp of red pepper flakes

- a quarter cup of fresh parsley (chopped)

- Sea salt and black pepper (freshly grounded)

Instructions:

1. Get the oven to 350° Fahrenheit before you begin.

2. Place the bell pepper halves in a 9x13-inch size baking dish.

3. Heat the olive oil in a big skillet over average temperature. Stir in the onion and garlic before you cook for five minutes, or cook until tender.

4. Include the quinoa, tomatoes, Italian seasoning, and red pepper flakes. Allow 5 minutes of cooking, stirring frequently.

5. Get it off the heat and add the parsley. Season with salt and pepper to get your preferred taste.

6. Fill each bell pepper half with the mixture of quinoa.

7. Bake for twenty to twenty-five minutes, or bake until the peppers are softened.

Prep time: 25 minutes | Serves: 8 | Calories: 106

Vegetable & Chickpea Stew

Ingredients:

- two tbsp of olive oil

- one diced onion

- two cloves garlic, minced

- two diced carrots

- two diced celery stalks

- one tsp of dried thyme

- one tsp of dried oregano

- half tsp of sea salt

- a quarter tsp of black pepper (freshly grounded)

- a quarter tsp of ground cumin

- one can (14.5 ounces) of undrained diced tomatoes

- two cups of vegetable broth

- one can (15 ounces) of drained and rinsed chickpeas

- two cups of chopped kale

Instructions:

1. Olive oil should be heated in a big pot over average temperature. Add the onion and garlic before cooking for five minutes, or cook until tender.

2. Stir in the carrots, celery, thyme, oregano, salt, pepper, and cumin. Cook for five minutes, stirring frequently.

3. Include the tomatoes, vegetable broth, and chickpeas. Bring to a boil, then bring down the heat to low before simmering for twenty minutes, or simmer until the vegetables are softened.

4. Add the kale and cook for another five minutes, or cook until wilted.

5. Serve and enjoy warm.

Prep time: 35 minutes | Serves: 6 | Calories: 204

Roasted Cauliflower & Red Onion Tacos

Ingredients:

- one head of cauliflower that's been cut into florets

- one red onion (cut into wedges)

- two tbsp of olive oil

- one tsp of chili powder

- one tsp of smoked paprika

- half tsp of garlic powder

- half tsp of sea salt

- twelve small corn tortillas

- a quarter cup of chopped fresh cilantro

- two limes (cut into wedges)

Instructions:

1. Preheat oven to 400° Fahrenheit before you start.

2. Get the cauliflower and red onion on a big baking sheet. Drizzle with the olive oil and season with chili powder, paprika, garlic powder, and salt. Toss thoroughly to coat.

3. Give a roasting time of 25-30 minutes, or roast until softened and lightly browned.

4. To assemble the tacos, place a few pieces of the roasted cauliflower and onion onto each corn tortilla. Use cilantro and a squeeze of lime juice to top it.

5. Enjoy warm.

Prep time: 30 minutes | Serves: 6 | Calories: 165

Creamy Coconut Cashew Noodles

Ingredients:

- eight ounces of brown rice noodles

- two tbsp of coconut oil

- half cup of raw cashews

- a quarter cup of coconut milk

- one tbsp of freshly squeezed lime juice

- one tbsp of tamari

- one tsp of garlic powder

- a quarter tsp of ground ginger

- two tbsp of chopped fresh cilantro

- Sea salt and black pepper (freshly grounded)

Instructions:

1. Cook the noodles following package instructions.

2. Heat the coconut oil in a big skillet over average heat. Add the cashews and cook for three to four minutes, or cook until lightly golden.

3. Include the coconut milk, lime juice, tamari, garlic powder, and ginger. Bring to a simmer before cooking for five minutes, stirring frequently.

4. Stir in the cooked noodles and cilantro. Season with salt and pepper to get your desired taste.

5. Serve and enjoy your dinner warm.

Prep time: 20 minutes | Serves: 4 | Calories: 329

Zucchini & Mushroom Lasagna

Ingredients:

- two tbsp of olive oil

- one diced onion

- eight ounces of sliced mushrooms

- two cloves garlic, minced

- two tbsp of tomato paste

- one tsp of dried oregano

- one tsp of dried basil

- two cups of marinara sauce

- two big zucchini (sliced into thin rounds)

- two cups of ricotta cheese

- half cup of grated Parmesan cheese

- Sea salt and black pepper (freshly grounded)

Instructions:

1. Before you begin, set the oven to a temperature of 375°F.

2. The olive oil should be heated in a big skillet over average temperature. Add the onion and mushrooms before cooking for five minutes, or cook until tender.

3. Stir in the garlic, tomato paste, oregano, and basil. Cook for just a minute, stirring steadily.

4. Include the marinara sauce and give it 5 minutes of simmering.

5. Layer the zucchini slices, ricotta cheese, and mushroom sauce in an 8x8-inch size baking dish. Sprinkle with the Parmesan cheese.

6. Bake for twenty-five to thirty minutes, or bake until the zucchini is softened.

7. Enjoy warm.

Prep time: 25 minutes | Serves: 6 | Calories: 323

Baked Sweet Potato & Black Bean Burritos

Ingredients:

- two medium sweet potatoes (peeled and cubed)

- one tbsp of olive oil

- one diced onion

- two cloves garlic, minced

- one tsp of ground cumin

- one tsp of chili powder

- half tsp of sea salt

- one can (15 ounces) of drained and rinsed black beans

- half cup of salsa

- eight whole wheat tortillas

Instructions:

1. Set the oven to a temperature of 400°F beforehand.

2. Place the sweet potato cubes on a big baking sheet. Drizzle with the olive oil before seasoning with salt and pepper. Toss thoroughly to coat.

3. Bake for 25-30 minutes, or bake until softened.

4. Heat the olive oil in a big skillet over average heat. Add the onion and garlic and cook for five minutes, or cook until tender.

5. Stir in the cumin, chili powder, salt, black beans, and salsa. Cook for 5 minutes, stirring frequently.

6. Add the roasted sweet potatoes and stir thoroughly to combine.

7. To assemble the burritos, spoon a few tbsp of the sweet potato and mixture of black bean into each tortilla. Roll up and serve.

Prep time: 30 minutes | Serves: 8 | Calories: 212

Broccoli & Chickpea Buddha Bowl

Ingredients:

- two tbsp of olive oil

- one head of broccoli (cut into florets)

- two cloves garlic, minced

- half tsp of sea salt

- a quarter tsp of black pepper (freshly grounded)

- one can (15 ounces) of drained and rinsed chickpeas

- a quarter cup of tahini

- two tbsp of lemon juice (freshly squeezed)

- two tbsp of sesame seeds

- two tbsp of chopped fresh parsley

Instructions:

1. Set the oven to a temperature of 400°F.

2. Place the broccoli florets on a big baking sheet. Drizzle with the olive oil before you season with garlic, salt, and pepper. Toss thoroughly to coat.

3. Give it 20-25 minutes of roasting, or roast until softened.

4. Place the chickpeas in an average bowl. Add the tahini, lemon juice, and one tbsp of the sesame seeds. Stir thoroughly to combine.

5. Place the roasted broccoli in a big bowl. Top with the mixture of chickpea, leftover sesame seeds, and parsley.

6. Serve and savor warm.

Prep time: 25 minutes | Serves: 4 | Calories: 315

Recipes For Snacks

Zucchini Fries with Avocado Aioli

Ingredients:

- two large zucchinis (cut into thick slices)

- a quarter cup of all-purpose flour

- a quarter tsp of garlic powder

- a quarter tsp of paprika

- a quarter tsp of salt

- a quarter tsp of black pepper

- a quarter cup of almond milk

- one cup of panko breadcrumbs

For the Aioli:

- half avocado

- two tbsp of olive oil

- one garlic clove, minced

- two tbsp of lemon juice

- Salt and pepper

Instructions:

1. Get the oven to a temperature of 400 degrees Fahrenheit before you begin. Make sure to line a baking sheet with parchment paper.

2. In a shallow bowl, put together the flour, garlic powder, paprika, salt, and pepper.

3. In a different shallow bowl, pour the almond milk.

4. In a third shallow bowl, pour the panko breadcrumbs.

5. Dip the zucchini slices first into the mixture of flour, then the almond milk, and lastly into the breadcrumbs. Place onto the prepared baking sheet.

6. Give it 20 minutes of baking, or bake until golden brown and crispy.

7. For the aioli, put together the avocado, olive oil, garlic, lemon juice, salt, and pepper in a blender or food processor. Blend thoroughly until very smooth.

8. Serve the zucchini fries with the aioli on the side.

Portion Size: 4 servings

Prep Time: 10 minutes

Cook Time: 20 minutes

Calories: 211

Baked Sweet Potato Wedges

Ingredients:

- two big sweet potatoes (cut into wedges)

- two tbsp of olive oil

- half tsp of garlic powder

- half tsp of smoked paprika

- Salt and pepper

Instructions:

1. Get the oven to a preheated temperature of 400 degrees F. Endeavor to line a baking sheet with parchment paper.

2. Place the sweet potato wedges onto the prepared baking sheet.

3. Drizzle with olive oil, before you season with garlic powder, smoked paprika, salt, and pepper.

4. Give it 25 minutes of baking, flipping halfway through, or bake until crispy and golden brown.

Portion Size: 4 servings

Prep Time: 10 minutes

Cook Time: 25 minutes

Calories: 143

Kale Chips

Ingredients:

- one bunch of kale (stem removed and torn into bite-sized pieces)

- two tbsp of olive oil

- half tsp of garlic powder

- Salt and pepper

Instructions:

1. Set the oven to a temperature of 350 degrees Fahrenheit. Next, you should use parchment paper to line a baking sheet.

2. Place the kale onto the baking sheet that you have prepared.

3. Drizzle with olive oil, then season with garlic powder, salt, and pepper.

4. Bake for fifteen minutes, or bake until crispy and golden brown.

Portion Size: 4 servings

Prep Time: 10 minutes

Cook Time: 15 minutes

Calories: 91

Baked Plantain Chips

Ingredients:

- two ripe plantains that's been peeled and sliced into thin rounds

- two tbsp of olive oil

- one tsp of garlic powder

- one tsp of smoked paprika

- Salt and pepper

Instructions:

1. Line a baking sheet with parchment paper after preheating the oven to a temperature of 350 degrees F.

2. Get the slices of plantain onto the prepared baking sheet.

3. Drizzle with olive oil, and season with garlic powder, smoked paprika, salt, and pepper.

4. Allow a baking time of 15 minutes, flipping halfway through, or bake until crispy and golden brown.

Portion Size: 4 servings

Prep Time: 10 minutes

Cook Time: 15 minutes

Calories: 105

Roasted Chickpeas

Ingredients:

- one 15-ounce can of drained and rinsed chickpeas

- two tbsp of olive oil

- one tsp of garlic powder

- one tsp of smoked paprika

- half tsp of cumin

- Salt and pepper

Instructions:

1. Preheat the oven to a temperature of about 350 degrees F. Then, you should line a baking sheet with parchment paper.

2. Place the chickpeas onto the baking sheet that's been prepared.

3. Drizzle with olive oil, and season with garlic powder, smoked paprika, cumin, salt, and pepper.

4. Bake for 25 minutes. Alternatively, you should bake until crispy and golden brown.

Portion Size: 4 servings

Prep Time: 10 minutes

Cook Time: 25 minutes

Calories: 201

Baked Apple Chips

Ingredients:

- two big apples (cored and thinly sliced)

- two tbsp of olive oil

- one tsp of cinnamon

- a quarter tsp of nutmeg

- Salt and pepper

Instructions:

1. Preheat the oven to 350 degrees F before lining a baking sheet with parchment paper.

2. Place the slices of apple onto the prepared baking sheet.

3. Drizzle with olive oil, then season with cinnamon, nutmeg, salt, and pepper.

4. Bake for 15 minutes, flipping halfway through, or bake until crispy and golden brown.

Portion Size: 4 servings

Prep Time: 10 minutes

Cook Time: 15 minutes

Calories: 97

Edamame Hummus

Ingredients:

- one 15-ounce can of drained and rinsed edamame beans

- two tbsp of tahini

- two tbsp of olive oil

- two tbsp of lemon juice

- one garlic clove, minced

- Salt and pepper

Instructions:

1. Put together the edamame beans, tahini, olive oil, lemon juice, garlic, salt, and pepper in a food processor or blender.

2. Blend thoroughly until everything is smooth and creamy.

3. Serve and enjoy with vegetable sticks or crackers.

Portion Size: 4 servings

Prep Time: 10 minutes

Cook Time: 0 minutes

Calories: 213

Avocado Toast

Ingredients:

- two slices of whole wheat bread

- one mashed avocado

- one tsp of lemon juice

- Salt and pepper

Instructions:

1. To begin, get the bread toasted until lightly golden brown.

2. In a little bowl, mash the avocado with the lemon juice, salt, and pepper.

3. Spread the mashed avocado onto the toast.

4. Serve and enjoy!

Portion Size: 2 servings

Prep Time: 10 minutes

Cook Time: 5 minutes

Calories: 233

Lentil Tacos

Ingredients:

- one cup of cooked lentils

- half diced red onion

- one diced bell pepper

- one garlic clove, minced

- two tbsp of olive oil

- two tbsp of taco seasoning

- eight to ten small taco shells

Instructions:

1. In a big skillet over average temperature, heat the olive oil.

2. Stir in the red onion, bell pepper, and garlic. For about five minutes, sauté until tender.

3. Include the cooked lentils and taco seasoning. Stir thoroughly to combine. Cook until heated through, about three minutes.

4. Divide the mixture of lentil into the taco shells.

5. Serve with your most treasured toppings.

Portion Size: 4 servings

Prep Time: 10 minutes

Cook Time: 8 minutes

Calories: 263

Chocolate Peanut Butter Banana Bites

Ingredients:

- two big bananas, sliced into 1/2-inch thick rounds

- half cup of smooth peanut butter

- half cup of dark chocolate chips

Instructions:

1. To begin, line a baking sheet with parchment paper.

2. Spread the peanut butter onto the banana slices.

3. Place the chocolate chips onto a plate before microwaving for thirty seconds, or until melted.

4. Drizzle the melted chocolate onto the banana slices.

5. Place the baking sheet into the freezer for one hour, or until the chocolate is set.

6. Serve and enjoy!

Portion Size: 4 servings

Prep Time: 10 minutes

Cook Time: 1 hour

Calories: 293

Recipes For Desserts

Vegan Chocolate Mousse

Ingredients:

- two ripe avocados

- a quarter cup of cocoa powder that's been unsweetened

- two tbsp of agave nectar

- one tsp of vanilla extract

- a quarter tsp of sea salt

- Fresh berries for topping

Instructions:

1. Peel and pit the avocados, then place in a blender or food processor.

2. Stir in the cocoa powder, agave, vanilla and salt and blend until everything is smooth.

3. Spoon the mousse into individual dishes and top with fresh berries.

Prep time: 10 minutes

Portion size: 4 servings

Calorie count: 90 calories per serving

Coconut Ice Cream

Ingredients:

- one can of full-fat coconut milk

- a quarter cup of pure maple syrup

- two tbsp of coconut oil

- one tsp of pure vanilla extract

Instructions:

1. Place the coconut milk, maple syrup, coconut oil and vanilla in a blender and blend thoroughly until well smooth.

2. Move the mixture to an ice cream maker and freeze following the instructions from the manufacturer.

3. Serve and enjoy the ice cream immediately or transfer to a freezer-safe container and freeze for up to 1 month.

Prep time: 10 minutes

Portion size: 4 servings

Calorie count: 150 calories per serving

Apple-Cinnamon Oatmeal Cookies

Ingredients:

- two cups of rolled oats

- one tsp of ground cinnamon

- half tsp of baking soda

- a quarter tsp of sea salt

- half cup of almond butter

- a quarter cup of pure maple syrup

- a quarter cup of unsweetened applesauce

- one tsp of pure vanilla extract

Instructions:

1. Preheat the oven to a temperature of 350°F and line a baking sheet with parchment paper.

2. In an average bowl, mix together the oats, cinnamon, baking soda and salt.

3. In another bowl, put together the almond butter, maple syrup, applesauce and vanilla.

4. Stir in the wet ingredients to the dry ones and mix until well combined.

5. Drop the cookie dough by the tablespoonful onto the prepared baking sheet.

6. Bake for ten to twelve minutes, or bake until the cookies are golden brown.

7. Allow the cookies to cool for ten minutes before serving.

Prep time: 15 minutes

Portion size: 24 cookies

Calorie count: 75 calories per cookie

Banana-Cacao Smoothie

Ingredients:

- one frozen banana

- one cup of unsweetened almond milk

- one tbsp of raw cacao powder

- one tbsp of chia seeds

- one tsp of pure maple syrup

Instructions:

1. Place all the ingredients in a blender and blend thoroughly until everything is smooth.

2. Serve and enjoy the smoothie immediately.

Prep time: 5 minutes

Portion size: 2 servings

Calorie count: 150 calories per serving

Vegan Chocolate Cake

Ingredients:

- two cups of all-purpose flour

- one cup of granulated sugar

- half cup of unsweetened cocoa powder

- one tsp of baking soda

- half tsp of baking powder

- half tsp of sea salt

- one cup of unsweetened almond milk

- half cup of melted coconut oil

- two tbsp of apple cider vinegar

- two tsp of pure vanilla extract

Instructions:

1. Get the oven to a temperature of 350°F and grease a 9-inch size cake pan.

2. In a big bowl, put together the flour, sugar, cocoa powder, baking soda, baking powder and salt.

3. In a distinct bowl, mix together the almond milk, coconut oil, vinegar and vanilla.

4. Add the wet ingredients to the dry ones and mix thoroughly until just combined.

5. Pour the batter into the cake pan that you have prepared and give it 30 minutes of baking, or bake until a toothpick inserted in the center comes out neat.

6. Allow the cake to cool for ten minutes before serving.

Prep time: 15 minutes

Portion size: 10 servings

Calorie count: 300 calories per serving

Baked Apples

Ingredients:

- four cored and sliced big apples

- a quarter cup of raisins

- a quarter cup of chopped walnuts

- one tsp of ground cinnamon

- two tbsp of melted coconut oil

- two tbsp of pure maple syrup

Instructions:

1. Preheat the oven to 350°F and grease a baking dish.

2. Place the apples in the prepared baking dish.

3. Sprinkle the raisins, walnuts and cinnamon over the apples.

4. Drizzle the coconut oil and maple syrup over the apples.

5. Allow a baking time of 25 minutes, or bake until the apples are softened.

6. Serve and enjoy the apples warm.

Prep time: 15 minutes

Portion size: 8 servings

Calorie count: 140 calories per serving

Vegan Coconut-Lemon Pudding

Ingredients:

- two cans of full-fat coconut milk

- half cup of pure maple syrup

- two tbsp of cornstarch

- Juice of 1 lemon

- a quarter tsp of sea salt

Instructions:

1. Place the coconut milk, maple syrup, cornstarch, lemon juice and salt in a saucepan and whisk until well combined.

2. Cook the mixture over average temperature, stirring steadily, until it thickens and boils.

3. Remove the pudding from the heat and transfer to individual dishes.

4. Put the pudding in the refrigerator for at least two hours before serving.

Prep time: 10 minutes

Portion size: 4 servings

Calorie count: 250 calories per serving

Vegan Chocolate-Covered Strawberries

Ingredients:

- one cup of dark chocolate chips (vegan)

- one tsp of coconut oil

- one pint of washed and dried fresh strawberries

Instructions:

1. Get the chocolate chips and coconut oil into a microwave-safe bowl before microwaving for 30-second intervals, stirring after each interval, until the chocolate is melted and smooth.

2. Dip each strawberry in the melted chocolate and place on a parchment-lined baking sheet.

3. Refrigerate the strawberries for at least thirty minutes before serving.

Prep time: 15 minutes

Portion size: 24 strawberries

Calorie count: 45 calories per strawberry

Peanut Butter-Banana Ice Cream

Ingredients:

- two frozen bananas (cut into chunks)

- two tbsp of peanut butter

- a quarter cup of almond milk (unsweetened)

Instructions:

1. Place the banana chunks, peanut butter and almond milk in a food processor and blend until creamy.

2. Serve and enjoy the ice cream immediately or transfer to a freezer-safe container and freeze for up to 1 month.

Prep time: 10 minutes

Portion size: 4 servings

Calorie count: 130 calories per serving

Vegan Brownies

Ingredients:

- one cup of all-purpose flour

- half cup of unsweetened cocoa powder

- one tsp of baking powder

- a quarter tsp of sea salt

- half cup of melted coconut oil

- three-quarter cup of pure maple syrup

- two tbsp of unsweetened almond milk

- one tsp of pure vanilla extract

Instructions:

1. Preheat the oven to a temperature of 350° Fahrenheit and grease an 8-inch size baking pan.

2. In an average bowl, put together the flour, cocoa powder, baking powder and salt.

3. In a different bowl, mix together the coconut oil, maple syrup, almond milk and vanilla.

4. Stir in the wet ingredients to the dry ones and mix thoroughly until just combined.

5. Pour the batter into the prepared baking pan and bake for 20 minutes, or bake until a toothpick inserted in the center comes out clean.

6. Allow the brownies to cool for ten minutes before serving.

Prep time: 15 minutes

Portion size: 16 brownies

Calorie count: 150 calories per brownie

Recipes For Smoothies

Orange Carrot Smoothie

Ingredients:

• one cup of orange juice

• one large peeled and chopped carrot

• one banana

• half cup of ice

• two tbsp of ground flaxseed

• two tsp of honey

Instructions:

1. In a blender, put together the orange juice, carrot, banana, ice, flaxseed and honey.

2. Blend thoroughly on high speed until everything is properly smooth.

3. Serve and enjoy immediately.

Prep time: 5 minutes, Portion size: 2 servings, Calories: 140

Coconut Pineapple Smoothie

Ingredients:

• one cup of coconut milk

• half cup of frozen pineapple

• one banana

• a quarter cup of almond butter

• one tbsp of chia seeds

• one tsp of honey

Instructions:

1. Combine the coconut milk, pineapple, banana, almond butter, chia seeds and honey in a blender.

2. Blend everything on high speed until very smooth.

3. Enjoy immediately.

Prep time: 5 minutes, Portion size: 2 servings, Calories: 200

Green Detox Smoothie

Ingredients:

• two cups of spinach

• half peeled cucumber

• half avocado

• half cup of coconut water

• one tbsp of ground flaxseed

• one tsp of honey

Instructions:

1. In a blender, get the spinach, cucumber, avocado, coconut water, flaxseed and honey together.

2. Blend on high speed and make sure that everything is smooth.

3. Serve immediately.

Prep time: 5 minutes, Portion size: 2 servings, Calories: 160

Mango Hemp Smoothie

Ingredients:

• one cup of mango

• half cup of hemp milk

• one banana

• two tbsp of hemp hearts

• one tsp of honey

Instructions:

1. Put together the mango, hemp milk, banana, hemp hearts and honey in a blender.

2. Blend all the ingredients on high speed until everything is smooth.

3. Serve and enjoy instantly.

Prep time: 5 minutes, Portion size: 2 servings, Calories: 240

Blueberry Matcha Smoothie

Ingredients:

• one cup of frozen blueberries

• one tsp of matcha powder

• half cup of almond milk

• one banana

• one tbsp of chia seeds

• one tsp of honey

Instructions:

1. In a blender, get the blueberries, matcha powder, almond milk, banana, chia seeds and honey together.

2. Blend thoroughly on high speed until everything is very smooth.

3. Serve immediately.

Prep time: 5 minutes, Portion size: 2 servings, Calories: 180

Strawberry Coconut Smoothie

Ingredients:

• one cup of frozen strawberries

• half cup of coconut milk

• half banana

• two tbsp of ground flaxseed

• one tsp of honey

Instructions:

1. In a blender, combine strawberries, coconut milk, banana, flaxseed and honey.

2. Blend everything on high speed until smooth.

3. Enjoy at the moment.

Prep time: 5 minutes, Portion size: 2 servings, Calories: 200

Chocolate Avocado Smoothie

Ingredients:

• half avocado

• half cup of almond milk

• one banana

• two tbsp of cocoa powder

• one tbsp of ground flaxseed

• one tsp of honey

Instructions:

1. In a blender, combine avocado, almond milk, banana, cocoa powder, flaxseed and honey.

2. Blend everything on high speed until properly smooth.

3. Serve immediately.

Prep time: 5 minutes, Portion size: 2 servings, Calories: 240

Acai Berry Smoothie

Ingredients:

• half cup of frozen acai berries

• half cup of almond milk

• one banana

• two tbsp of chia seeds

• one tsp of honey

Instructions:

1. Put together the acai berries, almond milk, banana, chia seeds and honey in a blender and blend on high speed until everything is smooth.

2. Enjoy immediately.

Prep time: 5 minutes, Portion size: 2 servings, Calories: 180

Banana Oat Smoothie

Ingredients:

• one banana

- half cup of almond milk

- a quarter cup of rolled oats

- one tbsp of ground flaxseed

- one tsp of honey

Instructions:

1. In a blender, combine banana, almond milk, oats, flaxseed and honey.

2. Blend on high speed until all the ingredients become smooth.

3. Serve immediately.

Prep time: 5 minutes, Portion size: 2 servings, Calories: 250

Papaya Coconut Smoothie

Ingredients:

- one cup of papaya

- half cup of coconut milk

- one banana

- two tbsp of chia seeds

• one tsp of honey

Instructions:

1. Combine the papaya, coconut milk, banana, chia seeds and honey in a blender.

2. Blend thoroughly on high speed until everything is smooth.

3. Serve and enjoy immediately.

Prep time: 5 minutes, Portion size: 2 servings, Calories: 170

It has been demonstrated that those with Hashimoto's Disease benefit from following a vegan diet. You can have a balanced diet by choosing the correct meals that are both nourishing and delightful. You can still get all of the vitamins and minerals required to lead a balanced and healthy lifestyle by integrating plant-based proteins, healthy fats, and complex carbohydrates. You will live a better, happier life by making a few easy dietary changes.

CHAPTER 3

WEEKLY MEAL PLAN

N/B:

For *Prep Time, Ingredients*, and *preparation Instructions,* please consult the previous chapter.

Monday

Breakfast: Oats and almond butter porridge

Lunch: grilled Portobello mushrooms

Dinner: Mediterranean grilled eggplant & zucchini salad

Snacks: Chocolate peanut butter banana bites

Tuesday

Breakfast: Quinoa and apple breakfast bowl

Lunch: Soybean and vegetable stir-fry

Dinner: Curried lentil soup

Snacks: Lentil tacos

Wednesday

Breakfast: Coconut chia pudding

Lunch: Roasted kale and Brussels sprouts

Dinner: Roasted butternut squash & kale salad

Snacks: Avocado toast

Thursday

Breakfast: Baked sweet potato toast

Lunch: Baked sweet potato fries

Dinner: Quinoa stuffed peppers

Snacks: Edamame hummus

Friday

Breakfast: Avocado toast with hemp seeds

Lunch: Avocado and bean wrap

Dinner: Vegetable & Chickpea stew

Snacks: Baked apple chips

Saturday

Breakfast: Coconut and banana pancakes

Lunch: Mediterranean chickpea salad

Dinner: Roasted cauliflower & red onion tacos

Snacks: Baked plantain chips

Sunday

Breakfast: Tofu scramble

Lunch: Roasted vegetable quinoa bowl

Dinner: Creamy coconut cashew noodles

Snacks: Roasted chickpeas

When you have Hashimoto's Disease, eating a vegan, gluten-free diet can be an excellent approach to enhance your general health and wellbeing. It's crucial to prepare in advance and make sure you eat the correct foods. You can prepare scrumptious, nutrient-dense meals that are catered to your needs with a little forethought and imagination.

Laura Osmond

CONCLUSION

The goal of The Hashimoto's Cookbook For Vegans was to give you the crucial knowledge and recipes you need to manage your disease. You can enhance your general well-being and lessen Hashimoto's disease symptoms by making the proper dietary adjustments.

You can make sure you are getting the nutrients you need while avoiding any items that might result in inflammation or other side effects by adhering to the vegan Hashimoto's diet. Additionally, you can discover strategies for giving in to your cravings while still adhering to the rules of the diet.

This cookbook's recipes are made to support you in leading a healthy lifestyle and consuming all the nutrients your body requires. The recipes are simple to prepare and can be modified to accommodate any dietary requirements.

Finally, you can find solace in the knowledge that managing your condition with a vegan Hashimoto's diet is both healthy and sustainable.

Laura Osmond

I hope that this cookbook has been a valuable resource in helping you manage your illness and that you have enjoyed the recipes' combination of healthfulness and delectability. Have fun cooking!

Printed in Great Britain
by Amazon

36041825R00057